MULTIGRANULARITY SERVICE COMPOSITION : CONCEPT AND TECHNOLOGY

SAURABH RAWAT

This book is dedicated to all the readers who are enthusiastic and willing to learn the concept of service oriented computing

Contents

Foreword

Computers are some of the most versatile tools that we have available. They are capable of performing stunning feats of computation, they allow information to be exchanged easily regardless of their physical location, they simplify many every-day tasks, and they allow us to automate many processes that would be tedious or boring to perform otherwise. However, computers are not "intelligent" as we are. They have to be told in no uncertain terms exactly what they're supposed to do, and their native languages are quite unlike anything we speak. Thus, there's a formidable language barrier between a person who wishes a computer to do something, and the computer that typically requires instructions in its native language, machine code, to do anything. So far, computers cannot figure out what they are supposed to do on their own, and thus they rely on programs which we create, which are sets of instructions that the computer can understand and follow.

This book forms a valuable addition to the existing bucket of knowledge in the field of SOA. This is especially intended for university students and researchers.

Saurabh Rawat and Anushree Sah
Date: 25-11-2022

Preface

Web services are widely used nowadays in software applications, as they have become a standard and convenient way of accessing remote applications over the medium of the Internet. Web services are remote procedure calls. The work proposes an approach to evaluate the methodology of web service substitutability and composability. We all are aware of the fact that web services have transformed into a widely used industry standard, but at the same time, web services may also be unreliable, as the mesh of services has gotten more complex. Hence, finding other services substitutable for an existing one can result in increasing the uptime of the application. Discovering and implementing such applications, which are composed, of composable web services i.e where we use the output of one service as an input to another web service.

Saurabh Rawat

Date

25-11-2022

Acknowledgements

I would like to express my greatest appreciation to the all individuals who have helped and supported me throughout the book. I am thankful to my computer colleagues for their ongoing support during the project, from initial advice, and encouragement, which led to the final combination of this book.

I wish to thank my parents as well for their undivided support and interest who inspired me and encouraged me to go my own way, without whom I would be unable to complete my project.

At the end, I want to thank my friends who displayed appreciation to my work and motivated me to continue my work.

Prologue

This Book gives an overview of SOA architecture and applications. Systems are getting bigger and bigger than ever before. So complexity is also increasing with them. As said by Juval Lowey "Complexity increases exponentially with size". And systems need to be interconnected with each other. So for interconnecting these systems many concepts evolved and more will come as per the demands in future. "Like OO (Object Oriented) solved the problems of small-medium sized systems. CO (Component Orientation) solved problems OO couldn't on medium-large systems. Neither OO nor CO could cope with the problems of very large systems, systems of systems, or integration between systems. So SOA evolved. SOA attempts to solve problems OO and CO could not solve by raising the level of abstraction. It is an architectural style and a design principle for application development and integration. Or we can say it is a way of designing software systems to provide "services" to end-user applications or to other services. SOA is a natural evolutionary step to the object-oriented (OO), procedural, and data-centric approaches adopted for solution implementation till now.

Chapter 1 is about basic introduction of all technologies used in SOA.

Chapter 2 is about different technological terms- Soa, web services, cloud computing.

Chapter 3 discusses about Literature Review over this area of research.

Chapter 4 This chapter discusses Multilevel Composability Model for Semantic Web Services.

CHAPTER ONE

INTRODUCTION TO SOA

Web services are widely used nowadays in software applications as they have become a standard and convenient way of accessing remote applications over the medium of the Internet. Web services are remote procedure calls. The work proposes an approach to evaluate the methodology of web service substitutability and composability. We all are aware of the fact that web services have transformed into a widely used industry standard, but at the same time, web services may also be unreliable, as the mesh of services has gotten more complex. Hence, finding other services substitutable for an existing one can result in increasing the uptime of the application. Discovering and implementing such applications which are composed of composable web services i.e where we use the output of one service as an input to another web service.

Web services are programmatically accessed over the Internet using SOAP(Simple Object Access Protocol). Programmers can access data remotely without extracting it from HTML web pages or any protocols. Web services work well when deployed independently but to associate composability in our applications, the services require to have an inter-relationship among them and it is difficult to integrate web services. As WSDL files don't carry enough information to decide substitutability or composability, there arises a necessity for automation of these techniques to deduce this information. In practice, it is often insufficient, as the web service operation parameter types are simply strings, float, and integers. It cannot be straightly assumed from a WSDL file if the input string is a stock ticker or a town name etc. The goal defined in the paper is to bring to light the creation of applications that deliver new functionality by integrating web services. Integration indicates here that services should be compatible with each other and one can be substituted for another at a required phase of time and inputs and outputs can be transformed for achieving compatibility. For example, suppose that a blogger posts a local weather report from a home meteorological station. A weather application could notice this new information source and determine that it is (imperfectly) correlated with other weather data, perhaps after-transformations. If the primary weather service becomes unavailable, the application automatically converts the blogger's information into a form compatible with the application and uses it to approximate the missing information. As another example, the system could determine when multiple services provide interchangeable functionality and choose the one that is cheapest, fastest, or most accurate based on user preferences. Such substitutability improves system reliability.

The idea of service oriented architecture (SOA) settles the issue of cross-stage asset sharing. To guarantee the seclusion and reusability, the usefulness of singular administrations is regularly restricted, hence they should be composited to fulfill the unpredictable interest of clients. The boundless utilization of distributed computing advances the advancement of SOA. As the quantity of administrations develops dramatically, the gigantic administrations with comparative usefulness present new difficulties to the adequacy and proficiency of the current help piece strategies.

It has been a research center to discover a help synthesis arrangement as rapidly as could be expected, which has the best properties and furthermore fulfills every one of the practical necessities. The current help organization techniques incorporate the neighborhood determination, the worldwide improvement, the savvy advancement, and the comprehensive technique. The neighbourhood determination technique can just acquire a nearby streamlining arrangement, yet, its productivity is high.

The worldwide improvement strategy changes the worldwide assistance sythesis issue into the blended number straight programming issue, and it can get the arrangement with top caliber in a moderately brief time frame, in any case, it requires every one of the target capacities and imperatives to be linearized, which restricts the application partially. Albeit the astute enhancement technique additionally has a high productivity, it can just acquire the inexact ideal arrangement in view of its arbitrariness.

In addition, the comprehensive technique can acquire the ideal arrangement surely, in any case, its time intricacy is too high to ever be reasonable. The flood of applicant administrations is the most significant factor to diminish the effectiveness of administration creation .

In the event that we can choose the expected administrations ahead of time, the inquiry space can be decreased and the effectiveness will be improved adequately. The idea of Skyline first showed up in the field of information designing, which is an assortment of information that can't be overwhelmed by others. In light of this, we can choose the non-overwhelmed administrations from each assistance bunch, at that point simply composite them to improve the productivity.

Web Service Paradigm emergence was due to the network technologies' widespread development and the use of the web which is primarily the next step in an evolutionary implementation chain of distributed applications. There are multiple interoperability opportunities that are offered by web services such as e-learning, e-commerce, e-banking, etc.

The web services are basically defined as a software component with one or more transactions ranging from simple to complex. This definition is given by W3C. The components are basically published, discovered and are invoked across the web through the use of an Internet as a communication infrastructure and XML or pom-XML as a data format.

The evolution of Service-Oriented Computing (SOC) provides much more efficient software development methods for engineering and building new value-added and service-based applications. SOC is a computing paradigm that relies on fundamental elements like web services.

Technical and research advancements in Web services composition have been considered as to develop new service-based applications as an effective opportunity satisfying complex requirements efficiently and rapidly. The research paper presents a novel approach enhancing the composition of semantic Web Services.

With Web services, the Internet became a platform for easily integrated, self-describing, and loosely-coupled software components. An aggregation or integration of various services into

a larger business collaboration is/are referred to as services composition; that is the technique proposed to interact, interoperate and coordinate multiple services to solve a complex problem and provide new functions of service in general. This resulting composition may then again be offered as a new, now composite Web Service.

It is worth-noting that the term composition is also used to describe different viewpoints (i.e., processes) of aggregation of Webservices. The use of specialized composition languages promises advantages in simplicity of development, automation capabilities, and maintenance compared to the use of standard programming languages like C or Java.

WSDL (Web Service Descriptive Language) can only describe the signatures of provided operations, new semantic description languages (e.g., Web Ontology Language for Services (OWL-S) are thus proposed to enrich WSDL descriptions with new annotations and syntactic constructions allowing to describe quite richly dynamic and semantic aspects related to the invocation of operations offered by these Web services.

One of the essential advantages of the Web service paradigm is reuse. Web services, as presented, are conceptually limited to relatively simple features that are modelled by a collection of operations. However, it is necessary to build new applications by composing services to meet more complex requirements.

Composability is a sought-after property. Notwithstanding, while there is generally a natural comprehension of this idea, a clear definition has been much of the time missing. In this paper, the author has refined the idea of composability. It was considered composability to be a property of architecture not of systems. Also, authors prefer not to decrease composability to the functional specifications; rather, we are zeroing in on how composability impacts the non-functional properties, particularly the formed framework's continuous conduct, its unwavering quality, its security, and so on We see the benefit of our methodology in having a wide application space. It works for functional and non-functional properties, it might think about both, equipment and programming, and it permits for a portrayal of arrangement irregularities. there was a slight improvement since 1996.

CHAPTER TWO

CLOUD COMPUTING, WEB SERVICES, SOA

Web Services:

The past decade has seen a boom in implementation of Service Oriented Architecture (SOA) in the corporate world thus leading to a rise in web services on the Internet. SOA allows for access to services through application components to the user thus creating a demand for service oriented applications by software vendors on the Internet. Before SOA, services can be said to be the end product of an application development process and in SOA, services can be delivered individually or combined as a larger entity thus comprising of an application.

However, the rise in availability of these web services has a demerit of its own. There is no particular method or algorithm for efficient management of web service repositories. It is not an easy task now-a-days to accurately find a desired web service amongst the huge number of web services available on the internet in a short span of time. It has become a necessary requirement to precisely and efficiently find functionally similar or equivalent web services in this field of serviceoriented computing.

One such solution to this issue is provided via the concept of Clustering Web Services. It efficiently facilitates service oriented tasks such as service selection, service discovery, service recommendation and service composition. It is mainly due to its applicability and accuracy.

Traditionally, clustering approach was based on WSDL descriptions which relied heavily on service syntactic features only and did not consider the semantic features.

Web Service Discovery :

Web Service Discovery is the process of finding suitable web services for a given task to meet the requirements of the service requester.Web service discovery methods are mainly divided into two categories: One is based on semantics and the other is based on keywords. The Semantic Web community proposes solutions such as Semantic Markup for web services and Web Service Modeling Ontology.

Semantic markup is the utilization of a markup language like HTML to pass on data about the importance of every component in a report through appropriate choice of markup components, and to keep up complete division between the markup and the visual introduction of the components contained in the record while WSMO or Web Service Modeling Ontology is a reasonable model for applicable perspectives identified with Semantic Web Services. It gives an ontology based system, which upholds the sending and interoperability of Semantic Web Services.

The term composability appears mainly in two (partly intersecting) areas:

• Software engineering in general, with a focus in Object-Oriented Programming (OOP) and Aspect-Oriented Programming (AOP)

• Actual architectures and systems, e.g., plug and play.

The Web service composition alludes to the process of making a composite service offering another usefulness, from straightforward Web services, through powerful revelation process, combination and execution of these services in a particular request to meet a particular need. To execute Web services and their compositions, numerous languages have been proposed. These languages incorporate WSDL, OWL-S, XLANG, BPEL or WSCI.

In view of the variety of users, which largely are not inspired by similar highlights and don't have similar profiles (context, preferences etc), Web services should create variation instruments to give the users pertinent and versatile services. As per Dey et al, "context covers all data that can be utilized to describe the circumstance of an element. The last can be an individual, spot, or article pertinent to the association between the users and the application, including the users and the actual application". To guarantee this need, it is important to coordinate the context all through the entire Web services life cycle.

Numerous researchers propose their composition approach dependent on AI planning strategies, by portraying a Web service as an activity, which is determined by its preconditions and impacts. Besides, planning is an expensive computational methodology and the size of the information associated with the planning process over the Web, will be a lot greater than ones utilized in old style planning issues. Context data, which is the significant component to be considered during choosing and consolidating services, can expand the acknowledgment and the adequacy of composition. A service composition model that can coordinate, and utilize context data to determine the ideal part services of the composite services is as yet a progressing research issue.

Cloud computing and web services:

Cloud Computing is a new trend in information technology that is gaining a lot of attention from researchers. It provides an accessible, flexible, and scalable computing system over the internet for users. It enables them to use these resources remotely over the internet. Using these services, a lot of money is saved that was earlier spent to establish computing infrastructure and maintain it.

Different users have different requirements. A single service can't fulfill all the needs of a user. Based on these requirements, a combination of different services is required to perform the request. Many web services have similar functions but the thing that differentiates such services is the Quality of Service(QoS). This includes availability, response time, cost, etc. Higher the QoS, Higher the income of the service providers.

A composite service is the combination of services that are based on their metrics corresponding to their QoS. For this, we need a composition algorithm that will choose appropriate services to satisfy the user's demand. The approach for this algorithm is to evaluate all possible services and choose the best one. Also, the most important thing to take care of is the Service Level Agreement(SLA) which needs to be satisfied by the composition method. It is the level of service expected from the service provider. If not satisfied then he must compensate for the violation.

If there are n number of tasks and m number of services with the same functions, then there are m^n choices for service composition. The service composition problem is an NP-Hard problem.

There are many metaheuristic algorithms considered to find approximately optimal solutions in a limited time. To solve the above-mentioned problem some metaheuristic algorithms have been introduced. However, to achieve better performance, those algorithms are not sufficient. Multi-verse optimization(MVO) algorithms are also introduced to solve this problem. But it requires some improvements that are mentioned as follows. The traveling distance rate decreases linearly by iterations which is the first weakness of this algorithm.

• Cloud computing to become widely adopted by both the enterprises and individuals, so a key issue that needs special attention is security of clouds.

• In cloud platform the user identity could not be verified as easier than other platforms which led to a topic of research.

• The trustworthy of the users could not be maintained by the service providers, because anybody can register the trust cloud and access according to the trust scheme henceforth, we needed new algorithm.

• The cloud security mechanism must be reliable and less time Consuming and previous algorithms were time consuming which motivated us to evolve a new algorithm.

• To create a trust relation between client and cloud Providers.

• To ensure Security and data integrity for every user.

• Laid down the Foundation because building trust systems for cloud computing is necessary.

• To have an environment free from malicious users that has trust manipulation and management and reputation.

Distributed computing empowers the movement of sensible, strong and on-demand programming, appropriately, progressively more expert communities convey their organizations in the cloud. In the conveyed registering, programming and hardware are preoccupied as resources and packaged as organizations. For instance, a couple of models of organizations are proposed, which consolidates programming as a help (SaaS), stage as an assistance (PaaS), and structure as a help (IaaS). SaaS is a top model and allows applications passed on by outcast venders. PaaS is in the middleware and passes on organizations as configuration, programs, etc PaaS gives features arranged to customers and is more extensible what's more, versatile than SaaS. IaaS oversees hardware as an assistance and enables VM development features between has. A help is portrayed by two sections: viable and non-valuable properties. When in doubt, with respect to web administrations, non-valuable properties are for the most part suggested as nature of organization (QoS). The valuable property portrays nuances of name of the help, its limits, the space of the assistance, and so on QoS contains a couple of decides that portray utilities and accommodation of organizations, which recollect rules for response time, throughput, costs, and availabilities. An individual assistance may disregard to complete an unpredictable customer interest, organizations are made together in the current situation.Right when the course of action issue satisfies both the commonsense goals and upgrade of QoS likewise, it is known as a QoS-careful assistance blend issuet regular.

CHAPTER THREE

LITERATURE REVIEW

Literature review of different works done so far in this domain:

We are living in the world where in every 1 second million and billions of data is processed and refined so as to provide a quality service. User base in different firms share their data and activities to use the service and that data is processed so as to improve the services. As we are moving forward this also is a threat to the privacy of user data. Accessing data in local machine was good old times but these days user has a power to sync their data to the cloud so that he/she can use services remotely from anywhere around the world. This opens another pipeline for direct target to user data. So, it's important for the firms to adapt a proper user access control management system. This article revolves around different algorithms and techniques to improve the security and precision when accessing the services in cloud.

Trust Management is a term generally used in computing world where user's request the service access is verified. In order to access the data present in the cloud server, the requesting user must have rights and registered to the cloud. Only if the user is registered to the cloud and has rights to access, he/she will be able to access the data.

The Proposed trust management comprises of different stages based on their functions which they perform. The basic architecture follows a fixed bath where in the user request is taken and provided to the Location based Service Composition Framework and then forwarded to the trust management scheme where the real time service composition happens. The location-based Service Selection is configured with the real time service composition to provide the service from different servers.

General key-based authentication mechanism has been carried out in different cloud security system however endures with various sort of organization assaults. The cloud security mechanism should be dependable and less tedious. In key based confirmation system, the calculation of keys and check strategy takes additional time when the quantity of clients goes in millions. So the security component should be less tedious one to help higher throughput of the framework. The area subtleties of the client could be utilized as one of the supporting components in improving the exhibition of the cloud climate. A similar arrangement of administration might be conveyed at various areas and must be gotten by the area of the client where the area ID must be finished. When the dependable of the client is checked then the area data can be utilized to choose and make the necessary administrations at runtime.

SUMMARY

• For cloud computing to become widely adopted by both the enterprises and individuals, several issues have to be solved.

• A key issue that needs special attention is security of clouds, and trust management is an important component of cloud security.

• In this paper, the authors look at what trust is and how trust management can Increase Security.

• A proposed Algorithm is evolved for Trust Management.

• The proposed trust management scheme has used various parameters for secure cloud computing.

• The proposed trust management scheme has four stages namely:

• Multi-Attribute Hashing function,

• Signature Verification

• Real-time service composition,

• extended trust management scheme.

• The hashing function has used all the parameters like user id, cloud id, service id and location information.

• The signature verification is performed as reverse to the key generation mechanism. The received key is computed with the size and then manipulated accordingly.

• The trustworthy of each user in the cloud is maintained using the trust management scheme where the trustworthy of different users are computed in different way.

• We also used the access history of services and user, based on which a service is selected and trust computing is done.

• The proposed method has produced higher efficient results than previous methods.

In the paper Simulation and modeling of an improved multi-verse optimization algorithm for QoS-aware web service composition with service level agreements in the cloud environments:

Introduction: In the Improved Multi-verse Optimization(IMVO) algorithm proposed, A set of p best solutions is used to produce a new solution instead of a single best solution. The proposed approach is more effective concerning other methods especially for problems faced by service composition methods with SLA.

Contributions:

1. An algorithm based on genetic algorithms has been introduced for solving service composition problems with QoS and has been compared with other genetic algorithms like random selection and exhaustive search algorithms.

2. An orthogonal genetic algorithm has been introduced to solve service composition problems with QoS. The orthogonal design is used for the initial population in this algorithm. This algorithm has outperformed traditional genetic algorithms.

3. CloudPick was introduced in multiple cloud environments. It provides a repository of cloud services to use QoS of multiple clouds.

4. Operators such as probabilistic and chaos have been used to generate individuals in this algorithm.

5. An algorithm based on backtracking and genetic algorithms is used to overcome the weakness of traditional algorithms that were trying to solve this composition problem while satisfying SLA.

6. An algorithm which is called Social Learning Optimization has been introduced. This algorithm simulates the human intelligence evolution process and it has been used for solving cloud service composition with QoS.

7. An algorithm based on ant colony optimization has been introduced which uses the least number of clouds in distributed cloud environments while considering time and QoS.

8. A linear programming algorithm was used to select an appropriate service per request while satisfied QoS criteria.

Cloud computing is a new trend in the computing world that provides resources and shares services over the internet for users. Many web services have similar functions and different quality of service (QoS). So, an appropriate service composition method is required to assign a composition of services according to the user's demand. Also, SLA should be satisfied by the service composition method. Introducing an improved web service composition algorithm that could get higher QoS while also satisfying SLA requirements which is one of the main issues in cloud computing. IMVO algorithm is proposed to improve QoS while satisfying SLA.

Many web services have similar functions and different quality of service (QoS). Different users have different requirements. A single service can't fulfill all the needs of a user. Based on these requirements, a combination of different services is required to perform the request. Many web services have similar functions but the thing that differentiates such services is the Quality of Service(QoS). This includes availability, response time, cost, etc. Higher the QoS, Higher the income of the service providers. Also, the most important thing to take care of is the Service Level Agreement(SLA) which needs to be satisfied by the composition method. It is the level of service expected from the service provider. If not satisfied then he must compensate for the violation.

The objectives of this research are:

1. Propose an improved multi-verse optimization algorithm to solve the web service composition.

2. To evaluate all possible composition services and choose the best one.

3. Improve this algorithm in both exploration and exploitation stages.

4. Compare the results of simulations to show the difference between the proposed algorithm compared and other algorithms especially for service composition problems with SLA.

5. Consider a weighted summation of the QoS parameters given by the user's requirements as the objective function of the web service composition problem.

Advantages:

1. Increase in normalized Quality Of Service(QoS) in comparison with other approaches.

2. SLA constraints are followed which are beneficial for service providers.

3. Efficient for a large number of iterations.

4. A set of solutions is used to find the next best solution instead of a single best solution.

Disadvantages:

Few disadvantages of the proposed method are listed below:

1. These algorithms are a bit complex to implement.

2. Cross-stage sharing has been an issue in the assistance design.

Multi-verse and Improved Multi-Verse Optimization Algorithm:

The process of the original Multi-verse optimization algorithm(MVO) can be described as follows.

- First, the initial population is generated.

- Each individual is considered as a universe and population is considered as universes. The objects are the variables in each solution in this universe.

- According to this algorithm, larger universes tend to send objects to smaller universes to gain the status of stability.

- In this optimization algorithm, a large universe is defined based on inflammation rate.

  ○ The existence of a white hole is related to the inflation rate

  ○ The existence of a black hole has an inverse relationship with the inflation rate

  ○ Objects go from the white hole to the black hole

  ○ The objects of all universes can be substituted by universes with a better inflammation rate

In the proposed Improved Multi-verse optimization algorithm(IMVO) the following weakness of the original algorithm was improved:

Travelling Rate(TR): The TR in the case of the original algorithm, decreases linearly by iterations. It can be shown mathematically as $TR_{original}$ = 1- (Iter/Max_Iter). In the first iterations, TR is high and it decreases by iterations. In the proposed algorithm, TR is adaptive and can decrease rapidly when after several iterations, the best solution can't be improved more. In this algorithm, TR is repeatedly decreased by half when for some distinct iterations it could not find a better solution than the already best solution again & the final TR will be the minimum of all the TR corresponding to a solution.

Summary:

Cloud computing is responsible for the delivery of services to users over the internet. However, there are a lot of different services with similar functions along with different QoS levels. Thus, choosing the appropriate service from a set of services to satisfy the user's demand is tough. This paper introduced an improved multi-verse optimization algorithm(IMVO) which tends to solve the service composition. According to the results of simulations, the proposed algorithm proved to be superior when compared with other algorithms especially when service composition problems are considered with SLA constraints. A weighted summation of the QoS parameter defined by the user's requirements was considered as the objective of the web service composition problem. The results show an increase of QoS up to 57% in comparison with the other algorithms, especially for service composition problems with SLA.

Technique/ Method Used: Web-Service Composition

Algorithm Used: Multi-Verse Optimization Algorithm(MVO)

Results:

We have used 5 different scenarios to show the performance of the proposed algorithm. The numbers of services considered for these scenarios are represented as five different values 10, 30, 50, 70, and 90. The number of atomic services per set is considered as 200, 300, 400, 500, 600, 700, 800, and 900... The proposed algorithm is compared with the mentioned well-known algorithms, i.e. GA, PSO, GSA, MFO, MVO for service composition.

According to the figures, the proposed algorithm has a better performance compared with others. For a small number of services (E.g. 10) the performance of the proposed algorithm is the same as other algorithms but for higher dimensional, the differences between the QoS of the proposed algorithm from others are more obvious.

Technique Cloud Computing and GPS

Algorithms • Multi-Attribute Hashing function,

• Signature Verification

• Real-time service composition,

• extended trust management scheme.

Results To achieve the precision in the locations based cloud computing services and proper service compositions

Future Enhancement We can add time zone along with the existing location based algorithm to improve the accuracy.

Limitations It requires proper internet connection and it requires continuous location monitoring.

3. The details of work on "A Nonlinear Service Composition Methodbased on the Skyline Operator" are:

Motivation

• Success in the advancement of technologies like cloud computing, DevOps, Big Data and AI-ML have given service architecture an edge over the existing models.

- Though there were some flaws in the existing models, but they had many advantages too which helped in working forward for some improved ones.
- The Skyline method had a positive impact based upon on its first understanding and statistical data.
- The calculation of Skyline services were easily understood by graph i.e Response time vs Price and seemed to be effective.
- In context to the service composition method, skyline method and Bonmin method gave quite optimized solutions with good range of efficiency.
- The existing method and algorithms were also proposed which included AMPL modelling, DGABC algorithm, exhaustive method, and other optimization methods.
- The factors like time period, efficiency, effectiveness, complexity and optimization worked well with some and were a drawback for others.
- There will always be the possibility of improvement in the current service architecture models as services are growing exponentially.

Contribution

- The article had stated the problems and issues faced in the field of service architecture and had proposed solutions for the same through methods and solutions to provide optimization.
- It is also clear that there is need of increasing the implementation of cloud computing and other technologies so as to fulfil the growing number of services and demands.
- The proposed methods that could contribute towards the efficient solutions are nonlinear service composition method based on Skyline operator, open-source programming method i.e. Bonmin.
- Skyline is basically a collection of data that cannot be controlled or dominated by others.
- There are many algorithms and models under these two methods.
- Some of the already existing models and methods include local selection, exhaustive method, global and intelligent optimization.
- The aim of the methods is to increase resource sharing among many platforms, increase efficiency, ensuring modularity and reusability.
- This would help the customers to satisfy all their demands and to improve the service composability.

Problem Description

- Cross- platform sharing has been a problem in the service architecture.

- The functionality of the services is often limited, and it becomes difficult to ensure modularity and reusability to much extent.
- Low effectiveness and efficiency of the already existing services methods.
- The complex functionality of the service composition methods.
- Finding out the optimal service composition solution becomes very difficult as the number of services are growing very fast.

The main objective of the report is to devise optimal web service composition technique while ensuring quality of solution. Various sub-objectives are listed below:

- Promoting the use and implementation of cloud computing for the development of service-oriented architecture to increase resource sharing, reusability and modularity.
- Improving the existing service models and algorithms to satisfy the complex demands of the customers.
- Understanding and using nonlinear service composition method which is based on Skyline operator.
- Solving the service composition problem by Bonmin programming method.
- Improving the efficiency of service composition along with the quality using the proposed methods.

Advantages

Few advantages of proposed method are listed below:

- Advancing the utilization and execution of distributed computing for the advancement of administration situated engineering to expand asset sharing, reusability, and seclusion.
- Improving the current help models and calculations to fulfil the mind-boggling requests of the clients.
- Comprehension and utilizing non direct help creation technique which depends on Skyline administrator.
- Tackling the assistance organization issue by Bonmin programming technique.
- Improving the proficiency of administration creation alongside the quality utilizing the proposed techniques.

Disadvantages

Few disadvantages of proposed method are listed below:

1. These algorithms are a bit complex to implement.
2. Cross-stage sharing has been an issue in the assistance design.

3. The usefulness of the administrations is frequently restricted, and it gets hard to guarantee particularity and reusability to much degree.

4. Low viability and effectiveness of the all-around existing administrations strategies.

5. The mind-boggling usefulness of the assistance structure strategies.

6. Discovering the ideal help structure arrangement turns out to be exceptionally troublesome as the quantity of administrations are becoming quick.

Non-Dominate Algorithm

Non-dominate is a technique for making a decision about the mastery of the arrangements in the multi-target improvement issue. The nature of arrangements is assessed by non-rule arranging, to give a reference to evolution and selection. In this paper an improved algorithm is proposed for solving the skyline set.

Algorithm:

Input: Matrix A (It represents the QoS value of the whole services in a group, which has |N candidate| rows and |ATTRIBUTE| columns. |N candidate| indicates the number of the candidate services in the group.

|ATTRIBUTE| represents the number of attributes considered for each service.

Output: The Skyline service set Sky of this group.

Summary

1. The idea of administration piece can give the complex usefulness for clients.

2. As the inescapable utilization of distributed computing, the quantity of administrations develops dramatically.

3. It turns out to be harder to discover the ideal help structure arrangement rapidly.

4. This paper proposes a nonlinear assistance piece technique dependent on the Skyline administrator.

5. The Skyline administrator is to discover an assortment of information that can't be overwhelmed by others, which is utilized to prune the repetitive administrations to lessen the search space.

6. At that point the help organization issue is defined as a nonlinear whole number programming model by a numerical programming language (AMPL), and settled by the current nonlinear solvers Bonmin.

7. The investigations show that the proposed technique can viably improve the productivity of administration organization, while

guaranteeing the nature of arrangement.

8. With the improvement of distributed computing, the number of administrations is dramatically expanding, which brings new challenges for the current assistance arrangement innovation.

9. To discover a help service composition problem arrangement fulfilling every one of the utilitarian necessities as fast as could be expected, this paper proposes a nonlinear assistance arrangement strategy dependent on the Skyline administrator.

10. The ruled administrations in each assistance gathering would be sifted through by Skyline, which can decrease the hunt space and improve the productivity successfully.

11. At that point the service composition problem is defined as a nonlinear whole number programming issue by AMPL, and addressed by Bonmin.

12. The experimental results show that the proposed method can obtain the optimal solution similar to the exhaustive algorithm, and the efficiency is also excellent.

13. Therefore, the service composition method based on Skyline can significantly improve the efficiency of service composition.

In the next paper "Graph Planning Based Composition For Adaptable Semantic Web Services" shows:

1) Introduction

In this point of view, utilizing methods for context aware AI planning technique to Web services composition is the focal establishment of our work. For along these lines, we propose to abuse context data all through the entire Web services lifecycle: in the depiction, disclosure, composition (planning) steps. Besides, if the chosen formed Web service is not, at this point utilitarian, users can choose another created Web service from the rundown returned by our composition calculation.

2) Contribution:

• This paper proposed a semantic versatile Web services composition strategy dependent on semantic context-aware planning graph

• The improving of the AI planning graph with the ideas of semantic similitude connection and context likeness

• A Web service composition calculation dependent on the semantic context-aware graph

• A strategy for extricating the arrangement of positioned arrangements dependent on the semantic similitude joins framework which stores the semantic connections and their related scores, and the context comparability table which stores the scores of context similarity of each service with the users context

• The composition technique is made out of three phases. The first is the graph planning development dependent on the revelation and the determination of nuclear Web services which fulfill the user's context and his inclinations.

• In this progression, semantic relations among data sources and yields of Web services are misused to upgrade the planning graph with semantic data.

• The second step is the backward inquiry wherein a bunch of best formed Web services is extricated.

• The third one is to rank the arrangement of removed arrangements dependent on their semantic and context scores.

Motivation:

• Because of the massive variety of users, which for the most part are not intrigued by similar highlights and don't have similar profiles (context, preferences,...), Web services are not ideal for such use cases.

• Web services should create transformation systems to give the users applicable and versatile services.

• According to Dey et al, "context covers all data that can be utilized to portray the circumstance of an element. The last can be an individual, spot, or article pertinent to the collaboration between the users and the application, including the users and the actual application".

• Moreover, planning is an expensive computational methodology and the size of the information associated with the planning process over the Web, will be a lot greater than ones utilized in traditional planning issues.

• To guarantee this need, it is important to coordinate the context all through the entire Web services life cycle.

• Many analysts propose their composition approach dependent on AI planning strategies, by depicting a Web service as an activity which is determined by its preconditions and impacts

Problem Statement:

These days, there are websites utilized by a great many users, each for their very own utilization. Due to the variety of users, which by and large are not intrigued by similar highlights and don't have similar profiles (context, inclinations, and so on), Web services should create transformation instruments to give the users pertinent and versatile services.

With the assistance of context-aware semantic planning graph procedure for Web service composition, we can make a service offering another usefulness, from basic Web services, through powerful disclosure process, mix and execution of these services in a particular request to meet a particular need of the users. This way Web services will create transformation systems to give the users significant and versatile services.

Objectives:

• Using an ontology based context model for broadening Web services portrayals with data about the most appropriate context for its utilization

• To change the composition issue into a semantic context aware graph planning issue to construct a bunch of best made Web services dependent on the user's context.

• Using Semantic and contextual closeness scores to discover made Web services list.

• Calculate a score for every up-and-comer arrangement and a bunch of positioned arrangements is gotten back to the users

Advantages of the Proposed Approach:

Context data, which is the significant component to be considered during choosing and consolidating services, can expand the acknowledgment and the viability of composition. A service composition model which can coordinate, and utilize context data to determine the ideal segment services of the composite services is as yet a progressing research issue.

In the event that the chosen Web service is not, at this point useful, users can choose another made Web service from the rundown returned by our composition calculation.

Ontologies are a decent decision in displaying the semantics between the relations between context boundaries. Since Ontologies are dependent upon semantic Web languages that empower sharing, thinking and reuse.

Disadvantages of the Proposed Approach:

Web services are not entirely solid and they increment application uptime.

It requires a ton of information as information, complex issues require more calculation and seemingly forever is needed to build up an acceptable outcome

The exhibition can diminish radically if an excess of immaterial data is contained in the particular of a planning task.

5) Forward Search Algorithm:

• The forward search calculation is utilized to develop the context-aware semantic planning graph.

• Semantic connection among data sources and yields boundaries of Web services is abused to improve the planning graph with semantic data.

• This calculation takes ReqComp, R, O and CO as its data sources and gives a context-aware semantic planning graph G, a semantic connection grid SLM and a context comparability table CS as yields.

• Initially the context-aware planning graph G contains the layer 0 where the arrangement of activities A0 is unfilled and the suggestions set P0 addresses the underlying condition of the planning issue and contains the solicitation input boundaries.

• The graph G is iteratively extended until one of the accompanying halting conditions is fulfilled: the planning graph arrives at a level for which the arrangement of recommendations contains all users required yield boundaries or when the planning graph arrives at a fixed-point level where $A_{i+1} = A_i$ and $P_{i+1} = P_i$.

• For each layer i>0, new services are found from the storehouse of web services dependent on semantic coordinating between the services' info boundaries and the arrangement of recommendations on layer I-1, and the context similarity of the found services with the user's context.

Summary

This paper has its essential spotlight on the different perspectives that accompany the applications on the Web services. This paper proposes a context-aware semantic planning graph strategy for Web services composition.

We first utilize an ontology based context model for expanding Web services portrayals with data about the most appropriate context for its utilization. At that point, we change the composition issue into a semantic context aware graph planning issue to fabricate a bunch of best made Web services dependent on user's context. The development of the planning graph depends on semantic context-aware Web service disclosure. This permit, for each progression of the development, to add most appropriate Web services regarding semantic similarity between the services boundaries, and their context comparability with the user's context. In the backward hunt step, semantic and contextual likeness scores are utilized to discover formed Web services list. At last, in the positioning advance, a score is determined for every up-and-comer arrangement and a bunch of positioned solutions is gotten back to the users. In this paper, a composite Web service is applicable if its score is higher than 0.5. It directed a progression of analyses on a bunch of users to decide this edge. Users are fulfilled if the composite Web service score is equivalent or higher than 0.5. Setting wsem and wcontext to 0.5. It demonstrates that users are fulfilled since returned composite Web services are applicable to their practical and non-utilitarian necessities.

As fundamental commitments of this paper, we notice: (I) the improving of the AI planning graph with the ideas of semantic similitude connection and context comparability, (ii) a Web service composition calculation dependent on the semantic context-aware graph, (iii) a strategy for separating the arrangement of positioned solutions dependent on the semantic likeness joins lattice which stores the semantic connections and their related scores, and the context closeness table which stores the scores of context similarity of each service with the users context.

The experimenting continues to be in progress and strive to find a better and more efficient way to make Web services more composite. The article also provides the detailed algorithms used in the process and also the experiment performed along with results. As a conclusion, this approach is carried forward with the hope to make rapid progress in this domain.

In the next paper: "A Multilevel Composability Model for Semantic Web Services" shows:

INTRODUCTION

So, the paper "A Multilevel Composability Model for Semantic Web Services" provides us with model through which we can find out if the two web services can safely be combined, which will eventually help us in avoiding runtime failures. Along with the model many algorithms have been also proposed for checking composability.

What is Semantic Web?

When we request a web page, we get our web page in the form of HTML and our system just know how to display that, but imagine if our computers can understand the actual meaning of our request, this would help us to get more relevant results, as our request is not just subjected to keywords but also the underlying meaning too. This is what the new web is Semantic Web.

Web Services and Ontology are two concepts that are the main reason for enabling Semantic Web. Web services are the set of related functionalities that can be programmatically accessed through the web and Ontology is a formal description of knowledge as a set of concepts within a domain and the relationships that hold between them, unlike taxonomies or relational database schemas, for example, ontologies express relationships and enable users to link multiple concepts to other concepts in a variety of ways.

The landscape created by Semantic Web services has spurred several research issues and the one we are discussing in this paper is Service Composition- the process of combining different web services to provide a value-added service. In today's world combination of services will provide us better result and also help companies to save a lot of time and resources which will be spent on recreating a service and for this we need to check if the services can be composed or not and for that the paper has discussed four levels of composability rules:

1. Syntactic
2. Static semantic
a. Static Semantic of operations
i. Serviceability
ii. Provider and Consumer Type
iii. Category
iv. Purpose
b. Static Semantic of message
i. Data type
ii. Business Role
iii. Unit
iv. Language
3. Dynamic semantic (Business logic)
Refers to the outcome expected after executing given a specific condition
4. Qualitative levels

They've also given the concepts of composability degree and ʈ-composability to cater for partial and total composability.

The two algorithms that are discussed in the paper are:

1. Business Logic Composability: It calculates degree and checks if the composability rules are being followed

2. Composability algorithm: It gives degree of similarity of operations vertically composable with source operation

Later these algorithms are implemented with different scenarios and it is found that these algorithms are efficient enough to find whether services can be composed or not.

The main motivation of this article is to propose a set of algorithms which makes the process of adding semantics into the web an easy process, by this the large ratio of data available on the internet which now become understandable by humans can be understood with the help of machines helping the humans to grow and contribute to the society.

This research paper talks about the main impediment which comes in the way of understanding the large proportion of data on the web that has been termed as understandable now, and that is adding semantics.

Through this paper adding semantics to we, hence making The Semantic Web is talked about.

The semantic web is nothing but an extension of the World Wide Web through standards or rules set by the World Wide Web Consortium (W3C), with the simple goal of making the available data on the internet machine-readable.

Having semantics added to the internet gives the information a well-defined meaning and hence making it understandable to humans and custom developed applications.

The problem considered in the article is: -

The web is one of the most powerful tools to form a connection between the humans and the bank of information, but as the number of data sources and applications on the web has increased many folds it has become quite evident that it cannot sustain its growth in its present form. The main problem due to this is that a large ratio of data is now understandable by humans or custom developed applications. So, to solve this problem this research paper is based on how to add semantics to the web by which the machines will be able to understand and automatically process the data that they merely display at present. Adding semantics is also a huge problem which has been talked and tackled in this research paper. The Semantic Web is an emerging paradigm shift to fulfil this goal. It is an extension of the existing Web, in which information is given well-defined meaning

Objectives of this article: -

1. Developing a multilevel composability model for semantic Web services

2. To propose a composability model to ascertain that Web services can safely be combined, hence avoiding unexpected failures at runtime

3. To define a set of rules called composability rules, which specifies the constraints and requirements for checking horizontal and vertical composability.

4. To propose a set of algorithms for checking composability.

5. To implement the proposed set of algorithms in WebDG, a prototype for government Web services.

6. To perform a full analytical and experimental analysis to assess the performance of the proposed algorithms.

ADVANTAGES:

1. The proposed algorithm is scalable as it can compute composability checking time for a large number of operations.

2. Efficacy is more i.e., the usefulness of the algorithm to consumers.

3. Three avenues in the area of service composition that could benefit from checking composability is, composition analysis, automatic composition and operation outsourcing.

DISADVANTAGES:

1. Simulation testbed is required otherwise webDG will not work.

2. For performance analysis Dynamic semantics is a better approach but the paper focuses on static semantics ordering.

3. Solaris can be a better approach to the semantic environment.

The composability model is formulated as follows: "determine the set T of target operation op within the registry so that SO is vertically composable with op". For that purpose, the proposed algorithm browses the service registry that contains some set of operation that could be outsourced by a given source operation to check vertical composability of SO.

Maximum number of target operation is determined by max_target variable by user because number of target operation may be large. After computing the composability at each level, composability degree is determined.

get_weightR and get_weightL is used to get the weight of current rule and current level to check if the corresponding weight is positive because if the Plugin Pre rule is not satisfied then Plugin rule is necessarily satisfied and for that we need weight to be positive.

The composability algorithm returns a Boolean answer for whether the operation is composable or not. If the rule is not satisfied than logs containing the details can also be generated.

SUMMARY

"A Multilevel Composability Model for Semantic Web Services"-by Brahim Medjahed, Member, IEEE, and Athman Bouguettaya, Senior Member, IEEE.

Developed a multilevel composability model for semantic Web services. The model is defined by a set of rules called composability rules. Each rule specifies the constraints and requirements for checking horizontal and vertical composability and introduced the concepts of composability degree and "?" composability to cater for partial and total composability.

In order to overcome the shortcoming of the existed methods, a new algorithm is proposed in this paper which can deal with not only simple CR but also complicated CR. An ontology-based framework for the automatic composition of Web services. We present a technique to generate composite services from high-level declarative descriptions.

Composing Web services requires the description of each service so that other services can understand its features and learn how to interact with it and to evaluate the time for generating composition plans. We consider three execution times:

1. The first execution time includes mode, binding, and operation semantics composability.

2. The second execution time corresponds to message composability.

3. The last execution time corresponds to composition soundness.

Discovering dynamic semantics, semantic composability - static and dynamic composability of operations and messages, analytical model, and performance analysis.

The aim of proposed algorithm is to determine the set of all operations within the service registry that could be outsourced by a given source operation and provide an implementation of the proposed approach in theWebDG prototype and investigating the definition of an "optimization" model for composite services based on our quality of composition (QoC) parameters.

Technique/Method used- Performance analysis, theWebDG,

Algorithms used- Composability checking algorithm, B- composability

Results- Performed analytical and experimental analysis to assess the performance of our algorithms.

Future Enhancement- definition of behavioural rules to consider pre/postoperations during the composability process, define techniques for the automatic composition of semantic Web services.

Limitations- Automatic composition of web services is yet to be achieved using dynamic semantics and simulation testbed is also required, otherwise WebDG does not support the output.

6. The paper "Runtime Exceptions Handling for Collaborative SOA Applications" discusses

This paper concentrates on the cooperative capacity of administration based framework, particularly in the alteration instrument for runtime exemption taking care of.

Primary commitments:

(1) Self-adaptive exception handling architecture for services resource has been built.

Special case alludes to the administrations disappointment (blame), organize blunder or irregular occasions caused by asset or prerequisites changes. Absence of special case dealing with system, it will prompt these issues, for example, poor execution, asset squander, poor streamlined administrations and even disappointment. So benefits asset provisioning must have the capacity to effectively deliver. They ought to have versatile runtime special case ability.

(2) Runtime collaborative adjustment mechanism has been designed to deal with requirements and context changes.

Because of absence of considering time changes and coordinating technique amongst necessities and engineering, this paper propose a versatile approach with prescient control to put the prerequisites of issue space adaptively mapped to the runtime design of arrangement space. The approach can take in the model in view of wavelet change to anticipate the execution of administrations segment, and actuate necessities development or model change of engineering to accomplish runtime versatile capacity.

In this manner, modifying the runtime engineering to manage setting changes and settling hinder and fall with runtime special case taking care of have turned into the earnestly tackled issues.

General process for service-based software (SBS) generation is:

Delivering services resource→publishing services→selecting services→services collection (services official and blend).

It is like the waterfall display or blended arrangement mode between top-down and base best approach. Be that as it may, the process absences of runtime special case taking care of without beginning from the necessities to defeat the exemptions, services asset deficiency and setting changes

Therefore, setting up the immediate input channel from client prerequisites to services accumulation, and executing SOA runtime flexible exemption taking care of to manufacture cooperative SOA are the inspirations of the contemplating and noteworthiness.

Services asset provisioning has turned into the agreement of SBS improvement for industrialization. Presently information group of services figuring for the most part incorporates lifecycle arranging, asset creation, distributing, charging and administration of SBS. Industry and scholarly group generally concentrate on the services revelation and services structure, the beginning stage of research is to accept that services asset is sufficiently rich. Along these lines, if no services are accessible for a few sections, the application engineer can enlist them in the service agent's catalog and hold up until the point that the required services are accessible.

1. Define the problem considered in the article within 5 to 6 statements and list out any five objectives in the article

The main problem that this paper discusses is that it talks about Services and how this process can be optimized and it goes through two simple processes. One of the problem that this paper discusses is how can we, out of all accords, lessen the runtime exceptions that occur while resource management. The approach that this paper talks on this issue does the homework based on wavelet transform to predict the performance of services component. Another problem is that the lack of effective runtime exception handling solutions for SBS. Exception alludes to the administrations disappointment (blame), organize mistake or unusual occasions caused by asset or prerequisites changes. Absence of exception taking care of component, it will prompt these issues, for example, poor execution, asset squander, poor streamlined administrations and even disappointment. So benefits asset provisioning must have the capacity to effectively create. They ought to have versatile runtime exception ability.

The primary issue of the current SOA for the most part lies in:

1. Traditional SOA does not have runtime versatile managing instrument and ability to meet the runtime setting changes.

2. Lack of powerful runtime exception handling answers for SBS.

The present day offerings help is delivered before by administrations supplier. The procedure is loss of runtime special case adapting to thought. thusly, altering the runtime structure to adapt to setting modifications and settling hinder and deteriorate with runtime special case taking care of have end up being the desperately tackled issues.

By method for genuine time altering the runtime programming structure to adjust to the necessities and setting changes, programming contraption can ensure its execution under unique load on account of absence of stylish technique, an approach to versatile guide the necessities of bother space into structure advancement of answer region, it turns into a key issue.

1. Self-adaptive exception handling architecture is proposed for the model needed.

2. Runtime collaborative adjustment mechanism has been designed.

3. It is set to make the resource allocation an easier and more effective process.

4. The paper proposes methods that can better the traditional SOA does not have runtime adaptive regulating mechanism.

5. The paper talks on how we can increment the ability to meet the runtime context changes.

Administration virtualization is intended to shield the heterogeneous properties of IT asset. Programming deliberation articulation will be decoupled with solid IT asset to acknowledge semantic comparability mapping between web administrations of IT level furthermore, business practical necessities. With the guide of administration virtualization, dynamic customization of customized administrations asset is investigated to finish moment and on-request creation for unmatched administrations asset in runtime. These endeavors ought to repay the absence of on-request versatile administrations customization for look into group.

2. Explain any five advantages and disadvantages of the proposed method

The advantages of the proposed system are:

1. The customers need services and the services quench their thirst by letting them produce more of their data. It can change inactive administrations choice inadequacy that can't fulfill clients' needs.

2. Self-adaptive Custom Service Resources Optimization: In custom resource provisioning, improvement is made on selection and search capabilities for the service provisioning acts.

3. An active custom approach that would be personalized according to requirements fragments according to SOA would be made.

4. Self-adaptive customs and service aggregation is implemented and managed.

5. A restart and exception control monitor would hold the abnormal condition for user service.

6. The efficiency of the system would be improved.

The major profits that this particular model reaps are the following:

1. We propose a customized dynamic custom approach driven by prerequisites sections for administrations requester-driven SOA with

versatile instrument. It will strengthen current status for tweaked administrations asset without runtime on-request customization.

2. We have planned a full arrangement of design and execution including self-adaptive custom, administrations collection restart and special case dealing with screen for irregular instance of client administrations. Likewise, practicality and straightforwardness will be engaged.

3. Through some scientific techniques, for example, custom advancement calculation of administrations asset, special case dealing with capacity with flexibility will be worked to improve and amount administrations asset creation in runtime.

The disadvantages of the proposed system are:

1. For systems that are intensively using internet in their computer software system, the runtime adjustment is difficult.

2. Validity of predictive control is still an issue when it comes to models that are based on PAAS system because predictions are seldom not true.

3. The Platform dependency makes it difficult for cross platform services.

4. Lack of general method on how to adaptively map the requirements is a major issue.

5. Every time the services found are unavailable, the services restart and waste time.

This paper concentrates on the cooperative capacity of administration based framework, particularly in the alteration instrument for runtime exemption taking care of.

The major objective of the system is the Self-adaptive exception handling architecture for services resource has been built. Also important is the Runtime collaborative adjustment mechanism has been designed to deal with requirements and context changes. The system has a lot of advantages when it comes to the allocation of resources and management of user requirements at runtime. The customers need services and the services quench their thirst by letting them produce more of their data. It can change inactive administrations choice inadequacy that can't fulfill clients' needs. Self-adaptive Custom Service Resources Optimization: In custom resource provisioning, improvement is made on selection and search capabilities for the service provisioning acts. An active custom approach that would be personalized according to requirements fragments according to SOA would be made. Self-adaptive customs and service aggregation is implemented and managed. A restart and exception control monitor would hold the abnormal condition for user service. The efficiency of the system would be improved.

This system thus solves both the problem of:

(1) Self-adaptive exception handling architecture for active services resource provisioning has been built.

(2) Runtime adaptive adjustment mechanism has been designed to deal with requirements and context changes.

The paper "Hybrid Optimization Algorithm for Large-Scale QoS-Aware Service Composition" shows

Motivation for the Article:

The fundamental inspiration driving this paper is that there is no calculation or approach is available which fulfil the demand with ideal number of QoS and the utilization negligible number if the web Services. In the huge scale situations, where many specialist co-op give their web benefits yet with various estimation of their QoS. This has been the key inspiration for the analyst to create QoS mindful administration arrangement.

The problem of generating automatic compositions that satisfy a given request with an optimal QoS(Quality of Service) is a very complex task, especially in large-scale environments, where many service providers offer services with similar functionality but with different QoS. This has motivated researchers to explore efficient strategies to generate QoS-aware Web service compositions from different perspectives.

Contribution:

The article proposed a half breed calculation for creating the mechanized structure of Web administrations. By the assistance of this half and half calculation it creates semantic info yield based sytheses with the assistance ideal end-to-end QoS. It additionally improve the quantity of web administrations of the subsequent arrangement.

First of all for a given request the given algorithm generates a directed graph with the web service which can give the expected output for a given input. Then after generating the graph a search is performed in polynomial time in order to calculate the optimal QoS. This can be done with the help of the Dijkstras Algorithm.

After finding the optimal QoS then with help of hybrid algorithm we find the path which can use the minimum number of the web services is used.

CHAPTER FOUR

MULTILEVEL COMPOSIBILITY MODEL FOR SEMANTIC WEB SERVICES

ABSTRACT

This research paper is about integrating heterogeneous web applications using web services. A SOAP web service is being used to integrate applications like ASP.NET, Java and database. As usage of internet is expanding and the concept of web service is gaining publicity so there is a growing market demand for more cost effective and efficient heterogeneous enterprise applications. Web services opens new market to software vendors and these software vendors have an edge over other software vendors using old/traditional models. Even expensive software can be shared by many software applications as a service and hence making it more economical for customers to use it. This paper discusses about the design and implementation of database and then integration of ASP.NET application with database. Later on a SOAP web service is exposed which communicate with database and will then expose three methods to the java application. This java application is made using Servlet and JSP. The SOAP web service can now be used by any other application as per the need in future

1. INTRODUCTION

For meeting the growing demands of the business, information sharing from various heterogeneous sources is a challenging issue. This paper proposes an approach of integrating applications using SOAP web service.

Language for communication between web services and any application is XML(EXTENSIBLE MARKUP LANGUAGE). If format of xml generated is different for different applications then inbuilt XSLT transformation engine is used for mapping values. We have made case study of House Bidding in ASP.NET, MS SQL Server 2000, java, REST Web services and silverlight application. An abstract framework of the system we are implanting is shown next in below figure.

Database

ASP.NET application

SOAP WS

SILVERLIGHT application

REST WS

Java application

In this we do not consider REST web service and silverlight application, these two will be covered in our next paper with few more enhancements. This is just an approach to use web services in real world and is more widely used and accepted. The case study has not been built for a real client, but if developed further, it has a potential for commercial application and could be used in real world. 2. Evaluation and Analysis of Literature Read There are some terminologies or technologies we are using in our case study. After understanding these topics it will be easier to understand my work. SOAP (Simple Object Access Protocol) SOAP is a lightweight protocol for exchange of information in a decentralized, distributed environment. It is an XML based protocol that consists of three parts: an envelope that defines a framework for describing what is in a message and how to process it, a set of encoding rules for expressing instances of application-defined datatypes, and a convention for representing remote procedure calls and responses. SOAP can potentially be used in combination with a variety of other protocols; however, the only bindings defined in this document describe how to use SOAP in combination with HTTP and HTTP Extension Framework. SOAP Specification

• A structured message format

• A processing model providing separation between application and infrastructure related computing concerns.

• An error handling mechanism based on SOAP Fault messages

• An optional technique for describing and processing remote procedure call (RPC) messages

• "uniform representation of remote procedure calls and responses"

• An optional mechanism for data representation in XML (SOAP Encoding)

• Rules for how to exchange SOAP messages via HTTP (SOAP/HTTP Binding)

• SOAP messages are simple XML documents that contain two mandatory elements, the Envelope and Body, and one optional element, the Header.

3. Implementation

CASE STUDY HOUSE BIDDING SYSTEM: In this paper we have described our database, ASP.NET application for managing bids, SOAP web service, and finally java application that will consume this soap web service.

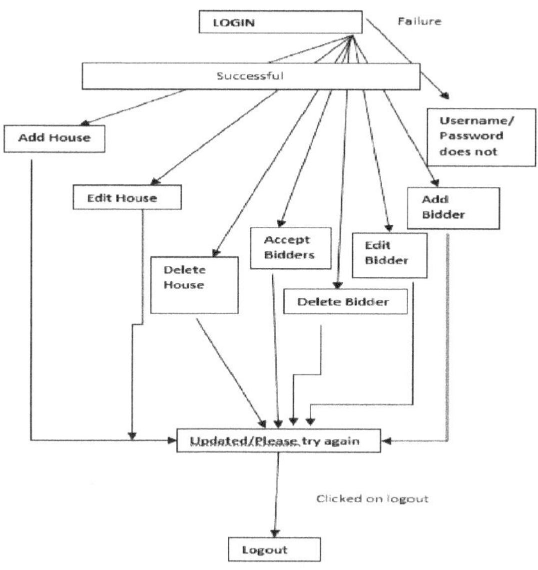

Fig 1. CASE STUDY HOUSE BIDDING SYSTEM:

4. CONCLUSION

In this chapter, on going work on the integration of heterogeneous web applications have been summarized. For doing so we have taken a case study House Bidding System. Firstly we have shown a figure which is an abstract framework that we are planning to construct. Then after this a case study is discussed, with its database tables, ASP.NET application, SOAP web service and Client Bidding (Java web application). This type of integration is most relevant for enterprise system implementation and for other forms of integration. Proper server side and client side validation will be done in the application. This application will prefer server side validation as client can deactivate client side validations any time and also because server side is more secure. As WWW is expanding and gaining publicity, so the scope of web services is also increasing exponentially. There are tremendous ways to use web services but we have discussed few ways of integration. In future, there can be more ways to integrate heterogeneous applications. These will be discussed in our next coming papers. In our further research, we will extend our architecture and will add REST web service and silverlight application.